Discard

Careers For People Who Like People

Interviews by Russell Shorto

Photographs by Edward Keating and Carrie Boretz

D0150331

CHOICES
The Millbrook Press
Brookfield, Connecticut

Produced in association with Agincourt Press.

Choices Editor: Megan Liberman

Photographs by Edward Keating, except: Anya Luchow-Liberman
(Carrie Boretz), Henry Richards (Jennifer Adams), Michael Krumper
(Carrie Boretz), Walter Martinez (Dean Jones), Pamela Waltz
(Carrie Boretz).

Library of Congress Cataloging-in-Publication Data

Shorto, Russell.
Careers for people who like people/interviews by Russell Shorto,
photographs by Edward Keating and Carrie Boretz.

p.   cm. — (Choices)
Includes bibliographical references and index.

Summary: People working in a wide range of careers, including day
care worker, flight attendant, and hotel manager, describe the
daily routine, benefits, and drawbacks of their jobs and the
education and training they received.

ISBN 1-56294-157-7
ISBN 0-395-63573-X (pbk.)

1. Vocational guidance — Juvenile literature.
2. Employees — Interviews — Juvenile literature.   3. Interpersonal
relations — Juvenile literature. [1. Vocational guidance.
2. Occupations.]
I. Keating, Edward, ill.   II. Boretz, Carrie, ill.
III. Title.   IV. Series: Choices (Brookfield, Conn.)
HF5381.2.S53   1992   91-27662
331.7'02 — dc20

Photographs copyright in the names of the photographers.

Contents

Introduction

In this book, fourteen people who work in people-oriented fields talk about their careers — what their work involves, how they got started, and what they like (and dislike) about it. They tell you things you should know before beginning a people-oriented career and show you how an enjoyment of being around people can lead to many different types of jobs.

Some of the careers in this book are in the service sector, such as hotel manager, flight attendant, and restaurant owner. Some — such as psychologist, school counselor, and child care consultant — involve interacting with people as an advisor. And others — convention organizer, sales representative, and publicist — utilize sales-related skills. Finally, some of the people profiled in this book work helping the public, such as the nurse, the cross-cultural counselor, and the city councilman.

The fourteen careers described here are just the beginning, so don't limit your sights. At the end of this book, you'll find short descriptions of a dozen more careers you may want to explore, as well as suggestions on how to get more information. There are many business opportunities for people-oriented people. If you enjoy this kind of work, you'll find a wide range of career choices open to you.

Joan E. Storey, M.B.A., M.S.W.
Series Career Consultant

"I don't just sit there, nodding. I prod my patients."

ANYA LUCHOW-LIBERMAN

PSYCHOLOGIST

Tenafly, New Jersey

WHAT I DO:

I'm a psychotherapist, which means that I counsel people. I do primarily crisis counseling. I don't deal with the chronically ill, but with people who were once able to lead their own lives yet are now facing a crisis. That crisis might be a divorce, a death in the family, or a move to a new town. But whatever the cause, it has made the patient so depressed and anxious that his or her problems suddenly seem insurmountable. At that point, they come to me.

Unlike an analyst, who might try to explore a patient's early childhood, a psychotherapist focuses on practical problem-solving. It's a hands-on approach. I don't just sit there, nodding. I prod my patients with questions and tell them what I

Anya tries to help her patients with their problems.

think. I might begin by asking, "Why are you here?" And then the patient tells me what he or she thinks the problem is. Sometimes, however, there is an underlying issue or a lifelong problem of which the patient is unaware. If there is, I deal with that issue, too. In the end, I try to develop the self-esteem of my patients so that they need not depend on a psychologist forever.

I'm in private practice, so about 70 percent of my week involves regular sessions scheduled in advance. The other 30 percent are crisis-oriented sessions and therefore unpredictable. For example, I might get a new patient whose distress is so great that I need to spend more time with this person than the usual forty-five-minute session. Or a woman may have just found out that her husband has been having an affair, and she needs more of my time. That's why, even when I go on vacation, I check my messages every day. I'm not like a physician who can have somebody else take over. I develop relationships with my patients, so another doctor just won't do. If someone feels distressed or is having a crisis, I have to be within reach.

I usually try to schedule about five patients a day. More than this is too stress-ful for me. You deal with a lot of pain in this job, and you can't make it all better. I'm in this line of work because I'm a people-oriented person, a problem-solver. I care, and I want to help. But it's also important to be careful that you don't become overwhelmed.

Anya makes notes after a session with a patient.

HOW I GOT STARTED:
I had a very strange path to this work. In college, I was a Russian major. Then I entered a Ph.D. program, intending to teach Russian literature. As part of the training for that, I had to spend time speaking with students who were having difficulty with their schoolwork. Often, they were also having problems with their lives.

Over time, I found that I was getting more satisfaction from helping them with their lives than I was from helping them with their work. I took a leave of absence to have a baby, and during that time I made the decision to change careers. I dropped Russian literature and instead got a master's degree and then a Ph.D. in counseling psychology.

HOW I FEEL ABOUT IT:
The worst part of this job is being unable to take someone's pain away. On the other hand, the best part is the

Anya usually sees no more than five patients a day.

incredible reward one gets from seeing someone become capable of leading a productive life. It's extremely satisfying when people say, "I couldn't have done it without you." I see myself as a support system — the scaffolding around someone who is wavering in the wind.

WHAT YOU SHOULD KNOW:
It takes a long time to prepare for this kind of career. You have to feel that this is really the work for you. If you're the person in whom all your friends confide their problems, if you're a listener,

then this may be the right field for you. But again, it takes time — first four years of college, then another one or two years in a master's program, and many more if you want a Ph.D.

A psychologist earns more than a social worker but less than a medical doctor. The money can be good, but most psychologists in private practice base their fees on a sliding scale that takes into consideration the patient's ability to pay. The standard fee now is between $90 and $100 per session, but I see some people for $20.

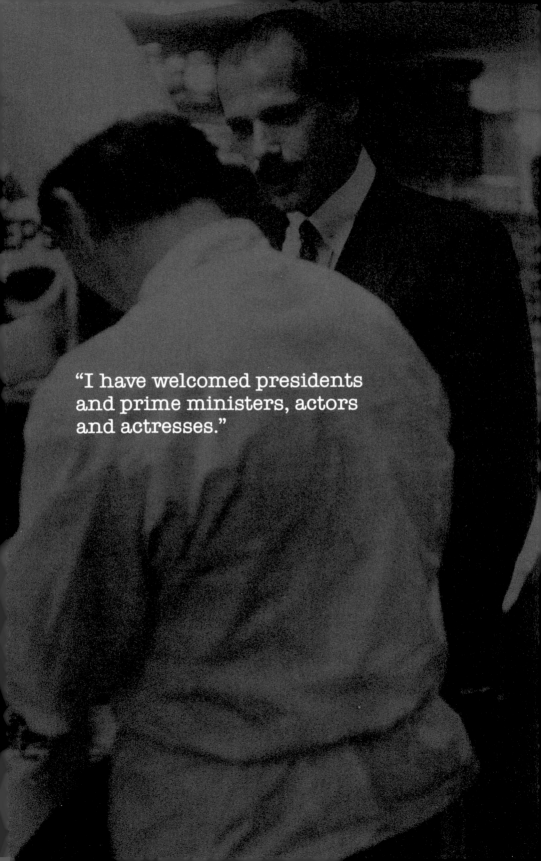

"I have welcomed presidents and prime ministers, actors and actresses."

DAVID KURLAND
HOTEL MANAGER

Coconut Grove, Florida

WHAT I DO:
I'm the general manager of the only five-star hotel in Florida, one of only eight five-star hotels in the entire United States. I oversee a staff of 350 employees who run the 181-room hotel. I'm also responsible for the daily well-being of my guests, which includes insuring friendly service, spotless rooms, and great food.

There's no typical day in the hotel business because each day is dependent on our interactions with the guests. Every morning, I meet with the front office manager and the room service manager to discuss the guests who will be arriving and whether any will be VIPs or special requests. Then, I meet with my assistant manager, and we discuss the operations project for that day, which might be the special cleaning of a section of the hotel or new flower arrangements for the lobby.

Meanwhile, I usually tour the hotel five to ten times a day. This means starting at the top and walking floor by floor down to the lobby. I inspect the restaurants, go into the kitchens and taste the food, and go into the lobby to meet the guests. I also oversee the marketing end of the business and control the budget.

HOW I GOT STARTED:
I studied psychology in school and worked in restaurants at the same time to make extra money. When I graduated, I became a child psychologist. But after practicing for a couple of years, I realized that I enjoyed the restaurant business more than I enjoyed psychology. So, I made the big decision to change fields.

David consults with one of the chefs at the hotel.

11

David tours the hotel five to ten times a day.

My first job in the hotel business was as the housekeeping manager of a hotel in New York City. Next, I worked as a director of catering, then as a director of sales and marketing. You tend to move around a lot in this business, and these jobs took me from New York to Philadelphia to Chicago and then back to New York. All the time, though, I was training myself in every aspect of hotel operation. Finally, I got the general manager's job here and moved to Miami.

HOW I FEEL ABOUT IT:
I couldn't imagine doing anything that would be more fun. I get to work in a beautiful environment. I get to eat great food and drink great wine. And this profession is not a sit-behind-your-desk one. It involves interacting with the guests and making sure people have a wonderful stay. Compliments are everything in this business. It makes you feel wonderful when people tell you that you have a great staff, that the service was perfect, and that they have never stayed in a better hotel.

My work is also very exciting because this hotel is so international. On any given night, there will be people staying here from all over the world, and I get to interact with them on a daily basis. I have welcomed presidents and prime ministers, actors and actresses to the hotel. On my walls, I have about fifty photos of famous people I have met here, including President Reagan, President Bush, Vice President Quayle, Boris Yeltsin, and Jesse Jackson. That's the colorful side of the job.

The one downside is that because the hotel never closes, the hours tend to be long. I usually arrive at 7:00 A.M. and leave about 7:00 P.M. I also work six days a week. And even when I go home, I still leave thinking about the hotel and the guests.

WHAT YOU SHOULD KNOW:
This is an industry that's a lot of fun, but it's also a lot of hard work. You have to enjoy being around people, but you also have to be service-oriented, outgoing, and experienced. Become as knowledgeable as you can about the outside world by traveling and going to school.

I'm a little different from most general managers in that I didn't go through hotel/restaurant school. That kind of program can give you a lot of the necessary background, but it's not a prerequisite.

The money is typical of most corporations. When you first join, the money isn't great, but as you move up it can be fairly lucrative. For the first few years, while you're proving yourself, the pay doesn't compare to that for someone coming out of law school. But as the years go by, you catch up. You might start out at $18,000 a year, but top pay is more in the area of $200,000 a year.

David reviews the guest list with a colleague.

"It makes me really happy when someone says the food is great."

KAREN GOLDBERG

RESTAURANT OWNER

San Francisco, California

WHAT I DO:

I own and operate an Italian restaurant. I run the business end as well as coordinating the five-person staff. I order, I cook, and I develop the menus. We've only been open for eight months, so right now we only serve breakfast and lunch. But we are planning to serve dinner, too, in the near future.

When you run your own small restaurant, you're always busy. I work seven days a week, twelve hours a day. I get in at six-thirty in the morning and set up for breakfast. This involves putting out the pastries we made the night before, making the coffee and fruit salad, and making sure the restaurant is clean and ready for the day's business. While we wait on customers during breakfast, we're also getting

Each morning, Karen prepares salads for the lunch crowd.

ready for lunch, making sandwiches and salads.

Meanwhile, all day long there are constant interruptions. People call about bills that have to be paid, for example, and I have to order food for the next day. It takes a tremendous amount of organization to run a place like this.

We have a big lunch rush from 11:00 A.M. to 2:00 P.M. During this time, I kind of shift jobs and become responsible for public relations. I mingle and talk with the customers, making sure everybody's happy. Then, when things die down around two, we start the clean-up in preparation for the next day's crowd.

The late afternoon is also a time when I try to think of dishes to add to the menu that are new and interesting. I try to keep up on trends in food, what's new and what's good. But while I'm creating

Karen makes sandwiches with one of her assistant chefs.

these new dishes, I always have to keep an eye on my budget.

HOW I GOT STARTED:

I had never been in the restaurant business before I opened this place, but I've always been interested in food. And after a trip to Europe not long ago, I fell in love with it. When I got back, I didn't know what I wanted to do. I'd been working in advertising, but I didn't want to do that anymore. Finally, I decided to open a restaurant. It's an incredibly hard thing to do, but it was what I really wanted. Then everything happened at once. I met the right people, and all the doors opened because I was doing what was in my heart.

Everybody said I was crazy to open a restaurant without any experience. Most places go under in their first year, or at least have to put up with big losses, but I've managed to make a profit every month after the first. I lost money the first month because I didn't know what I was doing. I was ordering the most expensive things — sundried tomatoes, imported everything. I wanted the best. But the products I was using were too expensive. Plus, I didn't understand how to manage employees. I was giving everyone free food. Once I learned those lessons, things got better.

HOW I FEEL ABOUT:

As hard as it is, I get excited every morning on my way down here because it's the right thing for me to be doing. I have always been a ham, a person who likes a lot of attention, and I get plenty of it here because I'm always dealing with the public. When someone says the food is great, it makes me really happy. I need that kind of positive feedback. But it's also very difficult, very challenging work.

There are bound to be people you don't get along with. You get your share of them in any business. But I've learned how to get along with them because I've had to. Working with the public is all communication. You have to learn to talk about what you're feeling. Because everything's so fast-paced, and there are a million things to do, there's no time to be anything but straightforward.

WHAT YOU SHOULD KNOW: Follow your heart. People may tell you that what you want to do is impossible, but don't listen to them. Take a risk. I did, and I don't regret it. The money will come by itself if you're doing something that you're really committed to.

Another important thing to know is that hard work will get you everywhere. You have to put your nose to the grindstone and be willing to work day in and day out for what you really want. There are a lot of different ways to go with your life. The important thing is, don't give up.

As far as earnings are concerned, in the beginning you're sort of paying off your investment, so you might make only $20,000 the first year. But once you get going, you have the potential to make $120,000, or even $220,000 down the line.

Karen waits on a customer during the breakfast rush.

"I've made friends from coast to coast."

HENRY RICHARDS

CONVENTION ORGANIZER

Pittsburgh, Pennsylvania

WHAT I DO:
I encourage organizations from around the country to hold their meetings and conventions in the Pittsburgh area. I work for the Greater Pittsburgh Convention and Visitors Bureau, which is a separate entity from the city. We're funded privately through membership and also by the state Department of Tourism. Our members are businesses in the area, mostly hotels and restaurants.

There's a lot of groundwork involved in this job. I have to target associations and study them until I come to understand their patterns — where they've met before and what time of year they normally meet. Then, once I know them, I can devise an approach in order to interest them in Pittsburgh.

Henry tells some convention planners about all that Pittsburgh has to offer.

When I get to work in the morning, I have a computer printout on my desk of the clients I need to contact that day. It lists their names as well as notes I've made to remind me why I'm calling them. I may want to follow up on information I've sent or to confirm a meeting. I spend a good part of the day making these calls so that I can keep in touch with clients and prospective clients.

My job also involves a lot of entertaining. Pittsburgh has suffered in the past from a bad image as a dirty steel town. But the city has gone through a revitalization, and my job is to show people the new Pittsburgh. I might fly in meeting planners from Colorado or Texas so I can show them the best our city has to offer. When they see the city for themselves, they're often surprised at what a fine place Pittsburgh is.

HOW I GOT STARTED:
I was raised here in western Pennsylvania, but I went to college out of state in Indiana. After college, I got my first job in Kansas. Then, I moved to Chicago, where I took a job with the Chicago Convention Bureau as a purchasing agent, buying everything from copiers to paper clips. In that job, I learned how a convention bureau works. Eventually, I talked my way into the sales department. Three years later, I got a call from a headhunter who was conducting a national search for the Pittsburgh bureau. I'm doing essentially the same thing here that I did in Chicago, but in Chicago I solicited corporate meetings, while here I work with trade associations and sporting events.

HOW I FEEL ABOUT IT:
This is definitely a people business. I interact with a lot of different people, both here and in my travels around the country. And I've made friends from coast to coast, so there is definite job satisfaction.

If there's a downside, however, it's that sometimes you have no control over when you have to travel. You might prefer to be at home, but suddenly you have to pick up and go. Also, the hours can be rough. We often have to do "fam" tours to famil-

Henry discusses plans with some convention organizers.

Henry reads about one of his clients' organizations.

iarize our clients with the city. When I'm conducting one of these, I'm with the client twenty-four hours a day to make sure they're comfortable and enjoying the tour.

During a "fam" tour, your life is not your own. I'll stay at the same hotel as my clients, give them my room number, and tell them to let me know if they need anything — day or night. You have to be there if they need you.

WHAT YOU SHOULD KNOW:
Convention and visitors bureaus are an entire industry unto themselves, and most people come to them from a hotel background. Many of these people have college degrees from hotel- and restaurant-management programs. A degree in hotel management would definitely get you in the door at a national hotel chain. Then, after a minimum of two to three years there, you could make the transition over to a convention bureau. I had a business and marketing degree, however, which was also helpful.

You won't get rich in this business, but you can be comfortable. Your first hotel job out of school will probably offer you a salary in the $22,000 range. However, since you'd be coming to a convention bureau with some experience, you might start out in the $25,000 to $30,000 range.

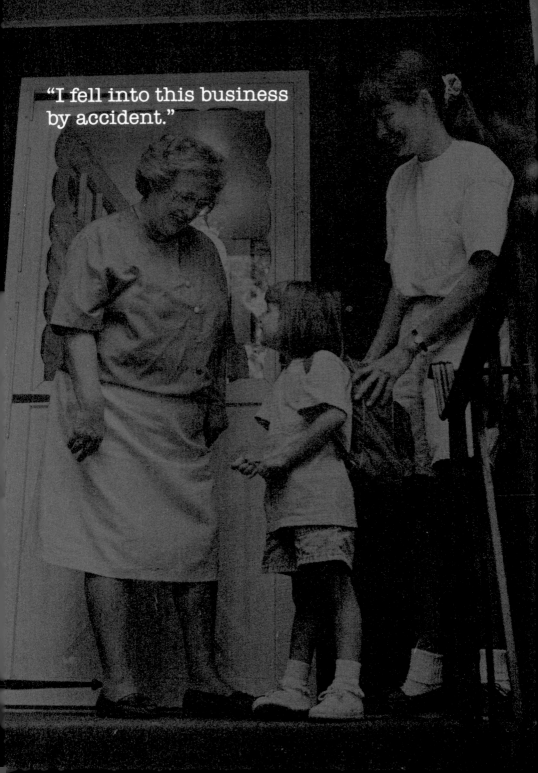

"I fell into this business by accident."

NAN HOWKINS
CHILD CARE CONSULTANT

Ridgefield, Connecticut

WHAT I DO:

I have several jobs, all of which are related to child care. One is administering a preschool. Another is administering a before-and-after-school program for elementary school students. I'm also a consultant who gives advice on how to set up and run child care centers. And I'm finishing a book on child care.

There's no set schedule in this business because you're dealing with people, and you can't predict what will happen. For example, in the child care center, we might have a child come down with a raging fever, or another will come in very upset because his or her parents are going through a divorce. You have to deal with these situations, and you never know what will come up.

Nan greets one of the young children under her care.

This is a very busy industry. When you have a quality preschool or child care center, people hear about it. Our center is well-known in the community. Even though we do very little advertising, we still have a waiting list for people who want to enroll their children here.

HOW I GOT STARTED:

I fell into this business by accident. I was a chemist working in cancer research when I realized that I enjoyed working with people more than I liked working in a lab. My children were young at the time, so I decided to open a preschool, as a hobby. Then, my husband lost his job, and we needed another source of income, so we branched out into child care. In time, we opened a second facility, then a third. Eventually, we had seven hundred children in our care on a daily basis.

Nan sits in on a class at the preschool she administers.

Once I got some experience, I found that my knowledge of the field was valuable. So, I set up a resource-and-referral service where parents and direct-care providers could call for assistance. We sponsor meetings and workshops, and we work with companies in the area who are considering setting up on-site day-care for the children of employees.

HOW I FEEL ABOUT IT:
I absolutely love my work. It's very fulfilling. But there are definite frustrations. A consultant is an advisor, and it's frustrating when someone doesn't take your advice about a program and you see it go down the drain. For example, one center hired a person who was an alleged child abuser. I suggested they fire this person immediately, but they said they couldn't do it because there were no grounds for dismissal – no proof – even though there had been charges at other centers where this person had worked. I finally walked away from the job, and this ultimately made them take action.

WHAT YOU SHOULD KNOW:
If you want to work in child care, find a volunteer position in which you can work with children of all ages. Learn which age groups you

like to work with best. Infant-toddler care is in the greatest demand, but not everyone can work with very young children. Then, explore career opportunities within child care. Find out what's available in your area. Are there more jobs in preschool or child care? Also, explore training options. The community college route is very popular.

If you decide you want to become involved with children on a long-term basis, you could become a teacher or an administrator. As a teacher, you work with kids. As an administrator, however, you don't have the same close contact. If you want to become an administrator, or own your own child care center, you must enroll in a degree program that has an administrative component. Most importantly, obtain as much hands-on experience as you can.

Starting out as an aide at a center, you will make minimum wage. As a teacher, you'll get an increase of about a dollar an hour, and a head teacher earns a dollar or two per hour more than a teacher. The salary for the director of a center might be as high as $40,000 a year. Owners make even more. There's no question this can be a very satisfying profession and a profitable business.

Nan plays with some children in the afterschool program.

"I don't go for creating news out of nothing."

MICHAEL KRUMPER

PUBLICIST

New York, New York

WHAT I DO:

Publicity involves arranging for media coverage for a particular product. As a publicist for a major record company, I approach editors of music and general-interest magazines to arrange for coverage of the artists on my label. I also try to get them coverage on television shows and arrange for bookings on national and local programs such as "Late Night With David Letterman" and the Arsenio Hall show.

Most mornings, I start work at ten. The workday at a record company is skewed much later than in a normal office because people often have to work at night. During a typical week, I might have to go to two or three concerts given by artists on the label, and these often run past midnight.

Michael arranges an interview with a musician on his label.

Much of my job involves doing publicity for artists on tour. I call newspapers and television stations in the areas where the bands will be playing to get advance stories on the shows. When you're calling these places, you have to know a lot about the artists in order to pitch them. You have to make them sound appealing. It helps to have a prepared sentence or two describing the kind of music they play and some additional information of interest.

Another aspect of my job involves interacting with the rest of the company. Once you've developed some press clippings, for example, you distill the best of them so the company can use the positive comments to market each artist's records. The marketing department will often use press quotes from an album review in a magazine or radio ad.

Michael talks to one of the musicians before the show.

HOW I GOT STARTED:

I was a premed student in college, where I also edited the music section of the student newspaper. As music editor, I dealt with the publicity departments of record companies who were trying to get me to cover their acts. Over time, I developed a relationship with someone at Elektra Records, and she offered me an internship there. Internships don't pay, but I did it for the experience — and also for the free records and the free admission to concerts. When you're young and in the music business, that stuff is really exciting.

I decided to put off applying to medical school for a year and instead got a job at a small independent publicity firm through someone I had met. I didn't like the place very much, but I learned the basics of publicity there. Also, through connections I made, I found another job. From then on, I didn't even think about medical school.

HOW I FEEL ABOUT IT:

An absolute pleasure of the job is getting to work with some wonderful musicians. I've met a lot of artists whom I really admire, such as David Crosby, Suzanne Vega, jazz legends like Don Cherry and Sun Ra, and bands I love like the Feelies. In publicity, you spend a lot of time with these people.

The job can have its routines, however. You make the same phone calls all the time, so it's a real challenge to make each group stand out. You have to pick your targets and be creative in your methods. You might take a group of writers out to lunch who you think are particularly appropriate to cover a story. Or you might bring an artist with an acoustic guitar over to a magazine office.

I once rented a rehearsal studio and had a guitarist play to show off for the editors of a couple of guitar magazines. But I don't go in for creating news out of nothing, which some people in the business do, such as making up rumors that some artist is dating another celebrity.

WHAT YOU SHOULD KNOW:
If you think you want to get into the music business, work for your college newspaper or your college radio station. You'll make contacts that will help you get internships. These internships are important because they get you into the business. Otherwise, you're just a name on a resume. The connections you make are invaluable because this is a real people-you-know business.

Publicity is not a very high-paying field unless you have your own independent firm. If you do have your own firm and you're very hot, you can charge $4,500 a month per artist for your company's services. But that's the top. Entering the business, your starting salary is about $20,000 a year.

Michael takes notes during a sound check at a club.

"Children can find in me
someone who will listen."

BEVERLY J. O'BRYANT

SCHOOL COUNSELOR

Washington, D.C.

WHAT I DO:
I work with students, parents, and members of the community to ensure the well-being of the students at my school. The programs that I supervise are designed to help students develop their educational, social, and personal strengths.

There are several basic tasks involved in counseling. To begin with, counselors are responsible for explaining to students, parents, and the school staff just what a guidance counseling program is. Much of what we do involves teaching life skills, such as how to get along with people and how to focus on your work. We also emphasize career issues, beginning with career awareness in elementary school and ending with career exploration and focusing in high school. In addi-

Beverly holds a group counseling session.

tion, we hold consultations with parents and teachers.

I've worked in an elementary school, a junior high school, a high school, and a kindergarten-through-twelfth-grade school, so I know counseling in all these areas. A typical day for me as an elementary school counselor might begin with walk-in counseling time, during which teachers, parents, and students can walk in and talk about whatever they want. Then, I might have a group guidance session with a class, in which I might focus on self-awareness or peer relationships. Following this might be a group counseling session focusing on a specific problem that had been identified by a teacher or by the students themselves. For example, I might talk about divorce to a group of students whose parents were all going through one.

Beverly discusses peer pressure with some students.

HOW I GOT STARTED:

I got my bachelor's degree in elementary education, and I worked for a few years as a teacher. But I soon realized that I was more interested in dealing with the problems that keep children from focusing on their work than I was in teaching, so I went back to school to get a master's degree in counseling. I learned that in many cases it was not teaching that was going to help students achieve. Rather, it was helping them learn to accept and understand themselves. Then they would be able to get on with their education.

HOW I FEEL ABOUT IT:

I love counseling. It is something that has a lot of intrinsic rewards. Children can find in me someone who will listen, and I find that rewarding as a human being. But this can also be a thankless job. People often put counselors in impossible situations because they don't understand what we do. Some school officials, for example, expect us to be adminis-trators, while some teachers look down on us because we don't have a classroom.

WHAT YOU SHOULD KNOW:

The way things are now, you

must have a master's degree to practice counseling. In the past, counselors were teachers. But now people realize that counseling is a skill for which you need special training.

Another thing you need for this kind of work is a friendly personality. You have to like people, be flexible, and be able to listen to others. You also have to be willing to continue the educational process. Once your master's degree is finished, you must continue taking classes periodically. The field of counseling is changing all the time, and you have to keep up with it.

The pay for a school guidance counselor is difficult to characterize because it varies from state to state. In general, a school counselor with a master's degree and a few years' experience can expect to make in the upper-$20,000 range.

Beverly looks over a student's file in her office.

"Nothing compares to the satisfaction you get serving at the local level."

WALTER MARTINEZ
CITY COUNCILMAN

San Antonio, Texas

WHAT I DO:

I'm currently serving my third two-year term in the San Antonio city council, which is an elective body of ten councilmen, each of whom represents a different district. The council's primary responsibility is to address the issues that govern the operation of the city. Together with the mayor, we set policy, adopt an annual budget, and direct the way the city provides basic services.

I represent an inner-city, low-income district that is 99 percent Mexican-American. The median family income in my district is about $14,000 per year. In one neighborhood, however, it's much lower, about $5,000 per year. My personal goal as a councilman is to develop and revitalize the community.

Walter discusses the budget at a city council meeting.

Young people need to realize that this sort of work is often not full-time. Serving on the city council in San Antonio is a part-time job. You have to complement it with your own career. Besides serving on the city council, I work for a local real estate company as a property manager.

My day is extremely busy. I schedule meetings starting at eight in the morning and don't usually return home until ten or eleven at night. I put in eighty-hour weeks, of which about forty-five hours are devoted to my work on the city council. A typical day might include a meeting with constituents at city hall, a school event, and a neighborhood association meeting in the evening. I might meet with a businessman who wants to open a store in my district and needs city help, or with a retired city employee having problems

35

Walter talks to constituents outside his office.

with his pension, or with someone complaining about a pothole on their street. Some visits are scheduled in advance; others are with people who just drop in because they see my car outside and know I'm here.

HOW I GOT STARTED:

I'm 40 years old now and have been involved in politics since I was 15. That was when my dad first encouraged me to work for the various local campaigns in which he was always involved. I later built on that experience by working for nine years as a legislative assistant in the state capital, serving the same area I represent today. Once I realized I liked this work, I began attending college part-time so that I could earn my degree. I knew that

to get ahead in politics I would need an education. In 1982, I ran for a seat in the Texas House of Representatives and won. But in 1984, I lost my bid for reelection. Later, I ran for the city council instead.

HOW I FEEL ABOUT IT:

Because I've had the opportunity to serve at both the state and local level, I'm often asked which I like better. Both are interesting and challenging, but there is no comparison with the satisfaction one gets serving at the local level. You're closer to your constituents and better able to see the fruits of your labor.

On the other hand, there are days when you ask yourself why you do it. You work a sixteen- or seventeen-hour day, and instead of a pat on the back, all you get are complaints. There's also a lot of frustration to be had in dealing with the system. Sometimes you feel like quitting. But you have to remember that every career has its frustrations.

WHAT YOU SHOULD KNOW: If you have any kind of interest in elective office, you should get an education. You should also be a sincere person and dedicated. People can tell whether you're serious about the pledges you make to improve the community. Also, you don't wake up one morning and say, "Today I'll run for city council." You have to be active in your community and develop roots there. You have to be willing to devote time and effort to improve the circumstances of the people who live there.

To find out whether you're interested in politics, it's a good idea to get some experience while you're young. Read the political columns in your local newspaper. Get involved in a local campaign. You can often do volunteer work for your city councilman or state legislator. I know I never turn away a volunteer, and there are even some students I'm able to pay a small stipend.

You can't support yourself on a councilman's salary alone. Councilmen get only $20 a week, plus $700 a month in reimbursable expenses. That's why you don't do this job for the money. You do it because you care about people, and you want to help your community.

Walter visits with some residents of his district.

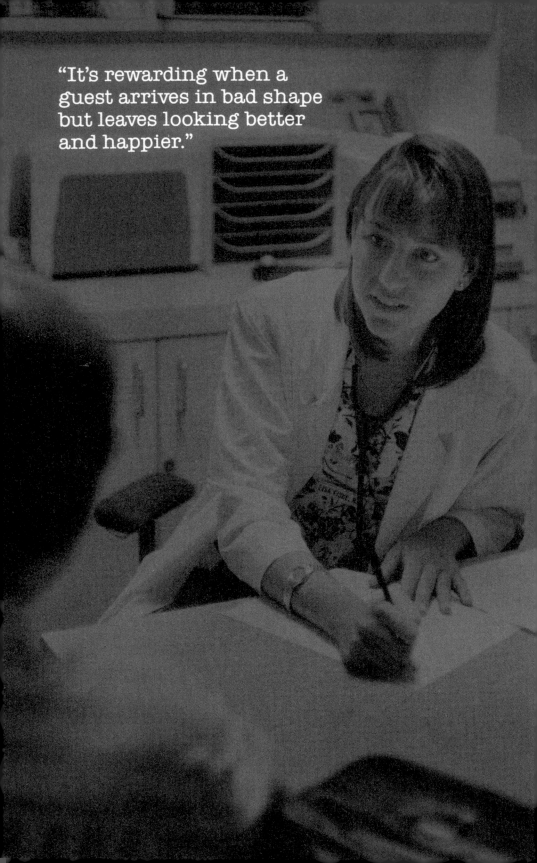

"It's rewarding when a guest arrives in bad shape but leaves looking better and happier."

LISA FISKE

NURSE

Miami, Florida

WHAT I DO:

I work as a nurse at a spa, which is a lot different from being a nurse in a hospital. People come to the spa to im- prove themselves. They want to become more fit or to lose weight. I screen all the guests when they check in to make sure they don't have high blood pressure or any other problems that might lead to an injury. I'm also here for minor emergencies — any- thing from a blister to some- one fainting. We have had all sorts of things happen that require a nurse.

Another important part of my job involves education. Some people who check in don't know about cholesterol or other basic health issues. I do a cholesterol screening of each guest and also a health-risk profile that compares each guest to the

Lisa makes notes for a health profile of a guest at the spa.

general population. These profiles can tell people whether they're at risk for, say, heart disease or cancer. I also draw blood and do a comprehensive blood analysis for guests who have high cholesterol or similar problems.

HOW I GOT STARTED:

When I began college, I majored in psychology because I knew I wanted to work with people. But then I discovered that nursing would give me an opportunity to work in several different areas, so in my third year I switched to nursing school. As a nurse, I can do physical therapy at a rehabilitation center, for example, or I can do work that involves psychology. If I had stayed a psychology major, my career would have been more limited.

At first, I wanted to work with children. So after graduating from nursing

Lisa discusses diet and exercise with some guests.

school, I took a job in pedi-
atric surgery at a hospital.
The hours were 7:00 P.M. to
7:00 A.M. — twelve hours
straight, all night long. It
was very stressful, partly
because of the long hours
but also because the schedule
varied. Sometimes I would
work Monday, Wednesday,
and Friday. Other times, it
would be different days. That
made it hard to plan ahead.
My entire life had to revolve
around the hospital.

After a while, I decided
I wanted a more normal
schedule. I got this job, and
I feel lucky. It utilizes the
same skills as a hospital job,
but it's less stressful.

HOW I FEEL ABOUT IT:
At a spa, you need personality
as well as skill. You have to
smile a lot. People are here to
have a good time. You don't
have sick people, but you have
people who want to improve
their way of life. They want
to exercise and to eat better.
I feel I'm helping to prevent
future problems.

I love my job. It's rewarding when you see a guest
arrive in bad shape but leave
a week later looking better
and happier. I have a favorite
quote that I keep on the wall
of my office: "Those who
think they have no time for
bodily exercise will sooner
or later have to find time for
illness." It's great when
guests who are out of shape
decide to start exercising. I
feel I've helped change them
for the better.

WHAT YOU SHOULD KNOW:

To become a nurse, you have to like the sciences, and you should have a real desire to do this kind of work. You have to want to work with people. You also have to go to nursing school, but if you don't like school, you can do a two-year program instead of a four-year program. As long as you pass your nursing boards, you're a registered nurse, or R.N. You can further your education later while you work.

In nursing school, you take basic English and math courses and so on. Then there is the nursing program, which involves rotations in medical-surgical, pediatrics, psychology, geriatrics, and labor-and-delivery. In each rotation, you study the subject in depth. That way, you can determine the direction in which you want to go.

There is money in nursing. To some extent, it depends on where you live. In New York, nurses make a ton of money. In Florida, base salary at a hospital is $13.52 per hour. If you work night shifts, you can make more. Working for a nursing agency, you can make from $20 to $25 per hour.

In a hospital, your salary increases regularly. If you stay in the same department long enough, you can become head nurse and make about $40,000 as base salary, plus extra if you work overtime. And the money is going up as the demand for nurses increases.

Working in a spa, you make less money because the work is less hectic. Starting pay is around $25,000, and you don't get regular raises the way you would if you worked in a hospital.

Lisa tests the cholesterol level of each new guest.

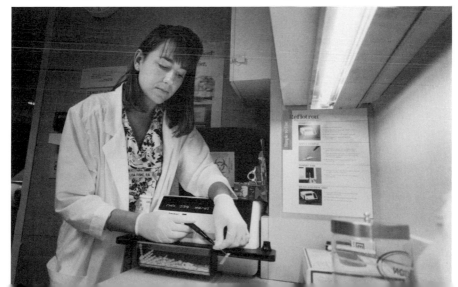

"In a desk job I'd feel restricted. Here I can do things my own way."

BILL GROVER

SALES REPRESENTATIVE

Mission Viejo, California

WHAT I DO:

I work for an independent rep company. We're the middlemen between manufacturers of audio and video equipment and the dealers who sell that equipment to the public. Manufacturers come to us and ask us to market their products, which we do through our distribution network of dealers. The manufacturers need us because we have a knowledge of the field, and because we've established a rapport with the dealers.

I usually start out in the morning touching base with several of the manufacturers we represent. I find out if they've encountered any equipment problems, whether any merchandise is going to be unavailable, whether there are new promotional campaigns to be implemented,

Bill is a middleman between manufacturers and dealers.

and so on. Then I look over my schedule for the day to see which dealers I'll be visiting. I usually call on five or six dealers a day.

When I visit dealers, I'm updating them on promotional programs, finding out whether they need any literature on the equipment, and handling any problems they might have encountered with our manufacturers' products. These are service calls. Another kind of call I make is to present a new product, which involves getting the dealer to stock that product and then training the dealer's staff.

HOW I GOT STARTED:

I moved from New Jersey to California in 1974. I had a two-year degree in liberal arts, and I saw an ad placed by an electronics company looking for manager trainees. I applied, got a job, and worked my way up to be a

Bill sells audio and video equipment to dealers, who then sell that equipment to the public.

manager in one of their stores. Then, I went to work for an audio manufacturer, first in sales and later as a product specialist training salesmen. But I eventually reached a point at which I wanted to get more involved with direct sales — I wanted to make commissions, instead of just a salary. So, I found this job, and I've been here for eleven years.

HOW I FEEL ABOUT IT:
I enjoy my work because it's diverse and fast-paced, and I'm someone who has to be constantly on the go. I guess I'd enjoy the security of a nine-to-five desk job, but I would feel restricted. Here, as long as I make my quota, I can do things my own way.

This business is always changing, and I like dealing with that. Right now, for example, some new companies are coming out with systems that tie audio and video together through a computer. You can watch a movie by tapping into a computer bank that will feed the movie into your system. This is a brand new thing, and we have to familiarize ourselves with it.

I'm also vice president of sales in my company, so I'm responsible for motivating other people. Dealing with people all the time has both a good and a bad side. Everybody is different. Some people won't listen to you; others are unhappy with the product or the service. In either case, you have to resolve the situation. But when you make people happy, that's great.

WHAT YOU SHOULD KNOW:
To do this job, you have to be patient, able to work with people, and able to meet deadlines. You also have to be able to understand what people want. Communications skills are very important in sales.

As far as education goes, take a course or two in advertising to familiarize yourself with the overall picture. An understanding of marketing and sales is also useful. I've worked in both manufacturing and retail, so I can understand the problems on both ends. It's not necessary to have practical experience in all facets of business, but it's good to get an overview so you can understand the other person's perspective. I think that holds true for any field.

The money in this business really varies. But I'd say that someone starting out as a sales rep would probably make about $35,000 a year. It's possible to make as much as $200,000, but not many people do. The average salesperson with a few years' experience is making somewhere between $50,000 and $55,000, but it always varies year to year.

Bill discusses a new speaker with a dealer he reps for.

"I feel I'm making a useful difference."

HELEN A. MENDES

CROSS-CULTURAL COUNSELOR

Culver City, California

WHAT I DO:
I specialize in both cross-cultural counseling and management consulting on issues related to cultural diversity. I have my own counseling center, where I currently have twenty-six professionals working for me on an as-needed basis.

Cross-cultural counseling involves talking with people of various races and backgrounds who may be having family- or work-related problems. We try to help these people solve their problems within the context of the values and traditions of their cultures.

Sometimes, people have difficulties that are directly related to being a member of a minority group. We help these people overcome their problems, such as low self-esteem, in two ways: We teach

Helen counsels people of diverse cultural backgrounds.

them to affirm their cultural roots and also to be aware of the effect that racism has had on them. For example, I have counseled black clients who grew up in families that believed light-skinned relatives were superior to dark-skinned relatives. I've also had Jewish clients who want their noses altered so they can look more gentile. These ideas are reflections of racism in the larger society that have been internalized by my clients.

We also do cultural-awareness training for corporations, teaching their managers how to be more sensitive to the needs of Asians, blacks, Hispanics, and women. For example, Mexicans believe it's a sign of respect to avoid looking a person in the eye. In our culture, however, we believe avoiding eye contact is shifty behavior. When we explain this sort of difference to the

Helen works with both individuals and corporations.

managers of a company, they acquire a better understanding of their employees.

HOW I GOT STARTED:

I grew up in a family with strong religious values. Even though we were poor, the value of helping others was always a part of my life. After college, I got a job as a welfare worker in New York City. I didn't like the bureaucracy, but I very much enjoyed helping people. Later, I got my master's degree and took a variety of other jobs in social work. Then I moved to California and worked as a teacher at the University of California at Los Angeles while I studied for my doctorate.

Around this time, I wrote *The African Heritage Cookbook*, which traced the development of soul food from sixteenth-century Africa to twentieth-century America. In doing the research for this book, I traveled to many parts of the world and gathered a great deal of information about different cultures. When I became a professor at the University of Southern California, I decided to specialize in cross-cultural social work.

Because my professor's salary wasn't enough by itself to pay my family's bills, I opened a private counseling practice on the side. Then, when the business grew quickly, I had to make a choice. I decided to leave the university and devote myself full-time to the business.

HOW I FEEL ABOUT IT:

I feel that I'm making a useful difference — not only in the lives of individuals, but in corporations as well — because I interact with high-level executives whose decisions affect the well-being of thousands of their employees. My work's also very challenging because it deals with racism. Not everybody we train is happy with what we're doing. Sometimes they bring discriminatory attitudes with them to the training, and it's a challenge to try to reach these people. Sometimes we do. Sometimes we don't.

WHAT YOU SHOULD KNOW: Study psychology and the social sciences. Also, learn about literature, history, and art. It's amazing how much those subjects come into play.

For example, it's sometimes possible to get an insight into a person from a character in a novel you once read. Or you might be able to help someone by discussing with them what was going on in the world while they were growing up.

Doing social work for a city government, you make about $35,000, depending on the city. Working for yourself, however, you can make hundreds of thousands of dollars. But to do that, you have to think like a businessperson and not like a social worker.

Helen counsels a young woman about problems at work.

"I'm totally addicted to what I do."

LUCIEN CHEREL

EMPLOYMENT MANAGER

Alexandria, Virginia

WHAT I DO:
I own an employment agency that matches certain types of companies with people looking for certain types of jobs. We have a staff of six at the agency, and we've been in business for sixteen years.

We specialize in technical fields such as banking, the environment, biomedicine, engineering, and data processing. I'm in the process of deciding whether or not to start a new company that will do nothing but science placements. That's where the growth has been recently.

During a typical day, I might conduct one or two interviews. When I give an interview, I try to find out what the person's skills are and what his or her background is. I ask the interviewees a lot of questions: What turns them on or off about a particular job? Do they want to change industries? Then I listen to their answers and determine which company to place them with. Later, I contact that company and tell them about the person's background. If they don't have any openings there, they may refer me to another company.

In addition to the interviews, I also have to take care of all the administrative work for the agency. I hate the paperwork — I'm a very unstructured person — but I've managed to work it out so that things get done without much fuss.

Finally, I visit a lot with the companies we've dealt with over the years, but not necessarily to do business. It may be just to ask how the company softball team is doing. This way, I can constantly keep in touch with their situation and their needs.

Lucien decides which people to place with which companies.

51

Lucien asks job applicants about their work experience.

HOW I GOT STARTED:
I started a translation company while I was still a business major in college in the Washington, D.C., area. I thought there was a need for translation work and also a need for an agency where translators looking for work could find it. I made some phone calls — and also some money — but in the end I found that I couldn't really make a go of it.

When I got out of school, a friend arranged an interview for me with an employment agency. I got the job and became the first person there to really focus on the banking field. I worked at that agency for a year and a half before deciding in 1975 to start my own firm. I had almost no money then, so I cut every corner. I even had a rotary dial phone because it was about eighty-five cents cheaper each month than a touch tone. I put every penny I had into the business, and we grew steadily.

HOW I FEEL ABOUT IT:
I'm totally addicted to what I do. I really look forward to

coming to work each day. But I love my weekends — I'm not a workaholic. In fact, I don't even get to work until 9:30 A.M. But I work hard when I'm here, and I expect to have a good day every day.

There's a necessary evil, however — a necessary part of getting started in this business — that I never liked. Your first year or two, all your work is solicitation — that is, getting your name in front of potential clients. At my first job, we were supposed to make a minimum of fifty calls a day to corporations. That was hard. It's much easier now, though, because I know the companies I deal with. Once you're on a first-name basis with your clients, the work becomes more comfortable, and your nucleus of clients becomes your living.

The stress is another problem with this business. There's a lot of money involved in each placement, so you feel a constant pressure to make it work. That's why they say most people in the industry burn out after three years.

WHAT YOU SHOULD KNOW: Business skills are important. So are psychological skills — the ability to read people in an interview, not just their words but how they choose their words and how they interact with you. Education is important because you have to be able to express yourself well and understand what people are talking about. Personality is also very important. You need to be someone people can talk to and someone who can listen.

The money is good in this field. I have a part-time person who makes more than $30,000 a year. Another employee of mine, who had never been in sales before he joined us recently, will make about $300,000 this year. The heaviest hitter that I'm aware of makes $500,000. And this is just an employment agency. An executive search firm makes even bigger money.

Lucien talks over a job placement at the agency.

"This job gives you not only the opportunity to travel, but also the time."

PAMELA WALTZ

FLIGHT ATTENDANT

Miller Place, New York

WHAT I DO:

My duty is to see to the safety and comfort of the passengers on board an aircraft, but really safety is the primary part of my job. Beyond that, I try to be sensitive to the individual needs of each passenger. You never know why people are traveling — whether for business, for pleasure, or for a reason that isn't happy — so you try to make sure that people are comfortable and have everything they need.

Flight attendants are based at a particular airport. I'm based at John F. Kennedy International Airport in New York City, so all of my flights start and end there. I fly domestic routes only. Most of my career has involved flights to San Francisco and Los Angeles, but my routes change each month.

Pamela arrives at the airport an hour before departure time.

My schedule varies, but it usually includes flights three or four days a week. I might start a trip on a Sunday with a flight to Chicago. I'll stay there at a hotel for sixteen hours, then fly to San Diego on Monday and back to JFK on Tuesday. Then I'm free until the next Sunday. During that time, I can pick up an extra trip if I choose to, but there's a limit to how many hours you're allowed to fly per week.

Flight attendants have a standard routine we follow when we're working. We have to be at the airport an hour or more before each departure. When we check in, we find out whether there will be any passengers on the aircraft, such as an unaccompanied child, who will have special needs. A half hour before departure, we board the aircraft and do a preflight safety inspection. We also make sure we have enough

Pamela waits for her flight in the attendants' lounge.

food and supplies on board as well as whatever special meals will be needed. Once the passengers board the aircraft, we make sure that everyone is safely seated, and then we prepare for takeoff.

HOW I GOT STARTED:

I originally wanted to be a nurse, and I went to a junior college for two years to study nursing. But I didn't like it as much as I though I would. Around that time, a friend suggested I apply to be a flight attendant. I did, I was hired, and the airline sent me to Chicago for special training. I started out based in Washington, D.C., then I was transferred to New York, and then to San Francisco.

Finally, I was transferred back to New York, where I've been ever since.

HOW I FEEL ABOUT IT:

In the beginning, it was rough because I was away from home all the time, and I got homesick. But now I really enjoy my work. I like meeting people, and I like the travel. I have friends all over the country, and my job allows me to visit them frequently. A nice fringe benefit is that my family gets to travel by paying only the tax on the fare.

Because of the schedule, you can do a lot of other things along with this job. A lot of attendants, for example, go to school. A few I know even went to law school while flying.

I have two sons myself, and I get involved with everything they do. Sometimes I switch around my schedule to be home for important events. But the hardest time for me as a mother is when my children are sick. The airline doesn't allow time off for that.

WHAT YOU SHOULD KNOW:
You have to be fairly easygoing in this job, and you really have to understand people. You come across all sorts of people in all kinds of different situations, and you have to deal with them. You should always have a smile on your face because people are always watching you — even when you don't notice. You also have to be willing to

relocate, at least when you're starting out.

Of course, you should like to travel. This job gives you not only the opportunity to travel, but also the time. For example, if you fly across the country and have a twenty-hour layover, you can rent a car and explore the area.

If you think you'd like this line of work, call an airline and ask for the in-flight services department, which will send you an application. The airlines like to see two years of life experience, either in a job or in college, but that's really the only set qualification.

The pay and benefits are good for the number of hours you work. A starting salary is about $16,000 to $18,000 a year. The top pay is probably about $45,000 a year.

Pamela checks to see whether any passenger needs assistance.

"You're always watching movies and talking about movies."

TOM BENTON

VIDEO SHOP OWNER

Hudson, New York

WHAT I DO:

My brother and I own and operate four video-rental stores. Because we're partners, we divide the responsibilities. I manage our twenty employees and handle the financial end of the business. My brother makes the daily rounds to the stores — carrying movies back and forth, picking up cash, and so on. He also does the legal work.

We started with one store in 1982 and added new stores in 1983, 1989, and 1990. Our main store is open from nine in the morning until midnight, so I typically put in a twelve-hour day. In the morning, I run a computer report on the previous day's rental activity. Then, I count up the cash, pay the bills, and order new titles.

Tom consults with a customer on movie selections in the children's section of his store.

HOW I GOT STARTED:

After I graduated from college, my brother and I got involved in raising cattle, but we soon tired of that. Then, we read an article in *Entrepreneur* magazine about the prospects for the video industry and decided to give it a shot. We started the business in 1981 with only $5,000.

At that time, nobody had ever heard of video rentals, and the business was slow to develop. But in 1985, the business really took off when there were finally enough VCRs in people's homes to create a market. It's been going strong ever since.

HOW I FEEL ABOUT IT:

This is a fun business because you're always watching movies and talking about movies. I also find working with the public very stimulating. I'm always speaking to people and getting feedback

Tom logs out a movie for one of his customers.

from them, hearing how they loved this movie or hated that one.

In a retail business, you have to be sensitive to your customers' needs. Early on, I asked my customers what they were looking for. They said they wanted a large selection of films, but also enough copies of new releases so they could rent the tapes right away. That's what I've given them.

Video is the kind of retail business in which you get a lot of the same people coming in time and again, so you develop relationships with them. This can be both good and bad. On the bad side, people sometimes give you a hard time and take their troubles out on you.

WHAT YOU SHOULD KNOW:
If you plan to start any kind of retail business, you ought to like dealing with people. Your entire livelihood depends on your customers. And you need to be willing to put in long hours in order to serve them properly.

At this point, the video marketplace is saturated. If you're going to get into it, you need a lot of money to establish yourself and obtain a share of the market. That can be a risky investment, however, because much of what we're doing now will probably be outdated in ten to fifteen years. Video is popular now as an entertainment medium, but it could soon be replaced by broadcasting.

As far as money goes, a single person operating one store might make between $30,000 and $50,000 a year if the store does well. A large, well-run store might earn the owner as much as $75,000 a year.

Related Careers

Here are more people-oriented careers
you may want to explore:

ARBITRATOR
Arbitrators work with companies
and individuals to settle disputes
when neither party wishes to take
the other to court.

CONCIERGE
Concierges work at the front desks
of hotels, supervising arrivals
and departures and providing
information to guests about where
to eat and how to get around.

**CUSTOMER SERVICE
REPRESENTATIVE**
Customer service representatives
respond to comments, questions,
and complaints from consumers.

DOCTOR
Doctors evaluate the health of their
patients and treat them for
illnesses.

FUND-RAISER
Fund-raisers solicit donations for
specific causes and projects, which
are often charitable in nature.

OMBUDSMAN
Ombudsmen investigate individuals'
complaints about misconduct on
the part of public officials.

SECRETARY
Secretaries handle correspondence,
scheduling, and other office work
that often involves interacting with
clients and colleagues.

TALK SHOW HOST
Talk show hosts interview guests
on radio and television programs.
They may also answer phone calls
from listeners and viewers.

TELEMARKETER
Telemarketers use the telephone to
sell goods and services and to
gather marketing information from
the public.

TOUR GUIDE
Tour guides lead groups of travelers
on trips all over the world. They
explain the history and culture of
the places they visit, organize
excursions to local points of
interest, and arrange for meals and
accomodations.

UNION ORGANIZER
Union organizers meet with non-
unionized workers to discuss the
pros and cons of forming a union.
If the workers vote to form a union,
then the union organizers help
them start one.

WAITER
Waiters work in restaurants taking
orders and serving food.

Organizations

Contact these organizations for information about the following careers:

EMPLOYMENT MANAGER
American Association for Counseling and Development
5999 Stevenson Avenue, Alexandria, VA 22304

HOTEL MANAGER
American Hotel and Motel Association
1201 New York Avenue, Washington, DC 20005

NURSE
American Nurses Association
2420 Pershing Road, Kansas City, MO 64108

PSYCHOLOGIST
American Psychological Association
1200 17th Street, N.W., Washington, DC 20036

SCHOOL COUNSELOR
American School Counselor Association
5999 Stevenson Avenue, Alexandria, VA 22304

FLIGHT ATTENDANT
Association of Flight Attendants
1625 Massachusetts Avenue, N.W., Washington, DC 20036

EMPLOYMENT MANAGER
Association of Human Resource Systems Professionals
P.O. Box 801646, Dallas, TX 75380

SALES REPRESENTATIVE
National Association of Professional Saleswomen
P.O. Box 2606, Novato, CA 94948

CROSS-CULTURAL COUNSELOR
National Association of Social Workers
7981 Eastern Avenue, Silver Spring, MD 20910

CHILD CARE CONSULTANT
National Childcare Association
1029 Railroad Street, N.W., Conyers, GA 30207

CONVENTION MANAGER
Professional Convention Management Association
100 Vestavia Office Park, Suite 220, Birmingham, AL 35216

PUBLICIST
Public Relations Society of America
33 Irving Place, New York, NY 10003

Books

CAREERS AND OPPORTUNITIES IN RETAILING
By Harriet Wilinsky. New York: E.P. Dutton, 1970.

CAREERS AND OPPORTUNITIES IN THE MEDICAL SCIENCES
By Arthur S. Freese. New York: E.P. Dutton, 1971.

CAREERS IN AIRLINE OPERATIONS
By Raymond Nathan. New York: H.Z. Walck, 1964.

CAREERS IN COUNSELING AND GUIDANCE
By Shelley C. Stone. Boston: Houghton Mifflin, 1972.

CAREERS IN ELECTIVE GOVERNMENT
By Robert V. Doyle. New York: Julian Messner, 1976.

CAREERS IN HEALTH CARE
By Rachel S. Epstein. New York: Chelsea House, 1989.

CAREERS IN SOCIAL WORK
By Frances A. Koestler. New York: H.Z. Walck, 1965.

CAREERS IN STATE AND LOCAL GOVERNMENT
By John W. Zehring. Garrett Park, Md.: Garrett Park Press, 1980.

CAREERS IN THE HOTEL AND TOURISM SECTOR
Geneva: International Labour Office, 1976.

CAREERS IN THE RESTAURANT INDUSTRY
By Richard S. Lee. New York: Rosen Publishing Group, 1990.

CAREERS WITH YOUNG CHILDREN
By Judith W. Seaver. Washington, D.C.: National Association for the
Education of Young Children, 1979.

HOW TO RUN YOUR OWN EMPLOYMENT AGENCY
By Paul Humphrey. Blue Ridge Summit, Pa.: Tab Books, 1982.

INTRODUCTION TO HOSPITALITY MANAGEMENT
By Kathleen M. Iverson. New York: Van Nostrand Reinhold, 1989.

INTRODUCTION TO HOTEL AND RESTAURANT MANAGEMENT
Dubuque, Ia.: Kendall/Hunt Publishing Co., 1984.

Glossary Index